Cursor from Zero to Hero

The Ultimate Guide to AI-Powered Coding

In this Book:

1. Introduction to Cursor

- What is Cursor?
- How Cursor enhances coding with AI
- Cursor vs. traditional code editors (VS Code, JetBrains, etc.)
- Installing Cursor on Windows, macOS, and Linux

2. Getting Started with Cursor

- Setting up your development environment
- Integrating Cursor with GitHub and repositories
- Understanding Cursor's AI features
- Customizing Cursor for efficiency

3. AI-Powered Code Assistance

- Writing and refactoring code with AI
- Generating functions and automating repetitive tasks
- Using AI to debug and optimize code
- Context-aware code suggestions

4. Working with Different Programming Languages

- Best practices for Python, JavaScript, TypeScript, C++, and more
- How Cursor adapts to different coding styles
- Using AI-generated documentation and comments

5. Enhancing Productivity with Cursor

- Using AI for test case generation
- Automating boilerplate code
- Managing large codebases efficiently
- Speeding up software development workflows

6. Advanced Cursor Features

- Real-time collaboration with AI-powered pair programming
- Customizing AI responses and settings
- Integrating Cursor with VS Code extensions
- Using Cursor for DevOps and automation scripts

7. Debugging and Optimization with AI

- Detecting and fixing bugs faster
- Performance tuning and code quality improvement
- Using AI to understand and analyze legacy code

8. Cursor for Web and Cloud Development

- AI-assisted front-end development (React, Vue, Svelte)
- Building full-stack applications with AI guidance
- Deploying projects with AI-powered DevOps suggestions

9. Real-World Projects with Cursor

- Building a REST API with AI assistance
- Automating unit testing and CI/CD pipelines
- AI-powered security analysis for code vulnerabilities

10. Conclusion and the Future of AI-Assisted Coding

- How AI coding tools are evolving
- Best practices for using AI responsibly in development
- Next steps: Exploring AI-driven software engineering trends

Cursor from Zero to Hero

The Ultimate Guide to AI-Powered Coding

Chapter 1: Introduction to Cursor

What is Cursor?

Cursor is an AI-powered code editor designed to enhance the software development experience by integrating artificial intelligence directly into the coding workflow. Built on top of **VS Code**, Cursor provides AI-driven code completion, inline suggestions, and intelligent debugging features, making it a powerful tool for both beginners and experienced developers.

Unlike traditional code editors, Cursor leverages AI models to understand the context of your code, offering suggestions, explanations, and even auto-generating boilerplate code. This significantly speeds up development, reduces errors, and improves overall productivity.

Key Features of Cursor:

- **AI Code Completion**: Predictive and context-aware suggestions while you code.

- **AI Chat Assistant**: Integrated chatbot to answer coding questions in real-time.
- **Automated Refactoring**: Helps in improving and restructuring existing code.
- **Intelligent Debugging**: AI-powered insights to detect and fix errors efficiently.
- **Code Documentation**: Generates explanations and documentation automatically.

How Cursor Enhances Coding with AI

Cursor takes coding efficiency to the next level by integrating **large language models (LLMs)** to assist developers in various ways. Here's how Cursor enhances the coding process:

1. **Faster Development**: AI-driven autocomplete and code generation reduce the time spent writing repetitive code.
2. **Fewer Errors**: AI-assisted debugging helps identify mistakes before they become major issues.
3. **Better Readability**: Cursor suggests cleaner, more maintainable code.
4. **Learning Assistance**: Beginners can benefit from AI-generated explanations, making it easier to understand complex code structures.
5. **Enhanced Productivity**: Developers can focus on problem-solving rather than syntax and boilerplate code.

Cursor vs. Traditional Code Editors (VS Code, JetBrains, etc.)

Cursor is often compared to traditional code editors like **VS Code** and **JetBrains IDEs (IntelliJ IDEA, PyCharm, WebStorm, etc.)**. Here's how Cursor stands out:

Feature	Cursor	VS Code	JetBrains IDEs
AI-Powered Coding	Yes (Built-in)	Requires extensions	Yes (Limited AI features)
Code Autocompletion	Advanced AI completion	Basic completion	Advanced completion
Integrated AI Chat	Yes	No	No
Automated Refactoring	AI-driven refactoring	Manual or extensions	Built-in but non-AI
Debugging	AI-assisted debugging	Traditional debugging	Advanced debugging
Code Explanation	AI-generated explanations	No	No

Cursor's integration of AI gives it an advantage in areas like automation, debugging, and learning assistance, making it a compelling alternative to traditional code editors.

Installing Cursor on Windows, macOS, and Linux

Installing Cursor is straightforward, and it supports all major operating systems. Follow these steps to set up Cursor on your machine.

Installing Cursor on Windows

1. **Download the Installer:**
   - Visit the official Cursor website: https://cursor.sh
   - Download the Windows installer (.exe file).
2. **Run the Installer:**
   - Double-click the `.exe` file.
   - Follow the on-screen instructions to complete the installation.
3. **Launch Cursor:**
   - Open Cursor from the Start menu or desktop shortcut.
4. **Sign in and Configure:**
   - Sign in with your GitHub or Google account (if required).
   - Configure AI settings and extensions.

Installing Cursor on macOS

1. **Download the Installer:**
   - Go to https://cursor.sh and download the macOS `.dmg` file.
2. **Install the Application:**
   - Open the `.dmg` file and drag the Cursor app to the Applications folder.
3. **Launch Cursor:**
   - Open Cursor from the Applications folder or use Spotlight (`Cmd + Space`, then type `Cursor`).
4. **Sign in and Configure:**
   - Sign in with your account and configure settings as needed.

Installing Cursor on Linux

1. **Download the Package:**
   - o Visit https://cursor.sh and download the Linux package (.deb or .tar.gz).
2. **Install the Package:**
   - o For Debian/Ubuntu-based systems, open a terminal and run:
   - o `sudo dpkg -i cursor.deb`
   - o `sudo apt-get install -f  # Fix dependencies if needed`
   - o For Arch Linux, install using AUR:
   - o `yay -S cursor-editor`
   - o For other distributions, extract and run the binary:
   - o `tar -xvzf cursor.tar.gz`
   - o `cd cursor`
   - o `./Cursor`
3. **Launch Cursor:**
   - o Run `Cursor` from the application menu or terminal.
4. **Sign in and Configure:**
   - o Sign in and set up AI features as required.

Post-Installation Setup

- **Extensions**: Install additional plugins for language support and AI customization.
- **Themes and Customization**: Modify themes and UI settings to match your preferences.
- **Keyboard Shortcuts**: Familiarize yourself with Cursor's hotkeys for faster navigation.

Conclusion

Cursor is a revolutionary AI-powered coding tool that simplifies and enhances the development process. By integrating AI features like code completion, chat assistance, and intelligent debugging, it stands out as a next-generation code editor. In the next chapter, we'll dive deeper into **Cursor's AI-powered features and how to use them effectively.**

Chapter 2: Getting Started with Cursor

Setting Up Your Development Environment

Before diving into the full capabilities of Cursor, it is essential to set up your development environment correctly. Follow these steps to ensure a smooth setup:

Step 1: Download and Install Cursor

1. Visit the official Cursor website and download the latest version for your operating system.
2. Run the installer and follow the on-screen instructions.
3. Once installed, launch Cursor and sign in or create an account if required.

Step 2: Configuring Cursor for Your Workflow

1. Open Cursor and navigate to **Settings**.
2. Choose your preferred theme, font size, and editor configurations.
3. Set up keybindings according to your workflow preferences.

Step 3: Installing Extensions

Cursor supports various extensions to enhance development. To install extensions:

1. Go to the **Extensions Marketplace** within Cursor.
2. Search for the extensions you need (e.g., Python, JavaScript, GitHub Copilot, etc.).
3. Click **Install** and enable them in your settings.

Integrating Cursor with GitHub and Repositories

Integrating Cursor with GitHub allows seamless version control and collaboration. Here's how you can do it:

Step 1: Connect Cursor to GitHub

1. Navigate to **Settings > Integrations**.
2. Select **GitHub** and click **Connect**.
3. Sign in to your GitHub account and grant the necessary permissions.
4. Once connected, your repositories will be available within Cursor.

Step 2: Cloning a Repository

To work with an existing project:

1. Click **File > Open Repository**.
2. Enter the GitHub repository URL.
3. Choose a directory to clone the repository and click **Clone**.
4. The project will now be available in your workspace.

Step 3: Committing and Pushing Changes

1. Make changes to your code within Cursor.
2. Open the **Source Control** panel.
3. Stage the changes and write a commit message.
4. Click **Commit & Push** to update the repository.

Understanding Cursor's AI Features

Cursor comes with built-in AI features designed to enhance productivity and streamline coding tasks. Here are some key features:

AI-Powered Code Suggestions

- Cursor provides intelligent code completions and suggestions based on context.
- Press Tab to accept AI-generated suggestions while coding.

AI Code Explanation

- Highlight any code snippet and use the **Explain Code** feature to get a detailed breakdown.
- This helps in understanding complex functions or debugging unfamiliar code.

AI-Powered Debugging

- Cursor can analyze errors and suggest fixes.
- Open the **AI Assistant** and describe the issue; the AI will provide potential solutions.

Customizing Cursor for Efficiency

Personalizing the Interface

- Adjust the **theme** and **editor settings** to match your preference.
- Enable **distraction-free mode** for focused coding sessions.

Setting Up Shortcuts

- Navigate to **Settings > Keyboard Shortcuts**.
- Customize keybindings to speed up common actions.
- Save and export your shortcut preferences for future use.

Configuring AI Behavior

- Go to **Settings > AI Preferences**.
- Adjust the level of AI suggestions (conservative, balanced, aggressive).
- Enable or disable auto-completions based on your workflow.

By following these steps, you will have a well-optimized development environment within Cursor, integrated with GitHub, and customized for efficiency. With AI-powered features at your disposal, you can write better code faster and with greater accuracy.

Chapter 3: AI-Powered Code Assistance

Artificial intelligence has revolutionized software development, providing tools that assist with writing, debugging, and optimizing code. AI-powered code assistants can significantly enhance productivity by automating repetitive tasks, generating functions, and offering context-aware suggestions. In this chapter, we will explore how to leverage AI to streamline the coding process.

Writing and Refactoring Code with AI

One of the most significant advantages of AI in software development is its ability to generate and refactor code. Developers can use AI-powered tools to write new code efficiently and improve existing code by optimizing structure and readability.

Benefits of AI-Assisted Code Writing:

- **Speed and Efficiency:** AI can generate boilerplate code, reducing development time.
- **Consistency:** AI enforces best practices, ensuring high-quality code.
- **Reduced Cognitive Load:** Developers can focus on logic and architecture rather than syntax.

Popular AI-Powered Code Assistants:

- **GitHub Copilot:** Suggests entire functions and automates code generation.
- **ChatGPT & OpenAI Codex:** Provides code explanations, generates snippets, and assists with debugging.
- **Tabnine:** Offers AI-driven code completions and contextual recommendations.

Example: Generating a Function with AI

Suppose you need a function to calculate the factorial of a number. Instead of manually writing it, an AI-powered tool can generate it instantly:

```
# AI-generated function for factorial calculation
def factorial(n):
    if n == 0 or n == 1:
        return 1
    return n * factorial(n - 1)
```

Generating Functions and Automating Repetitive Tasks

AI can be a powerful ally in automating repetitive coding tasks such as writing boilerplate code, generating unit tests, and creating API endpoints.

Automating Unit Tests

Manually writing unit tests can be time-consuming. AI-powered tools can generate test cases based on function definitions.

Example: Generating unit tests with AI for the factorial function:

```python
import unittest

class TestFactorial(unittest.TestCase):
    def test_factorial(self):
        self.assertEqual(factorial(5), 120)
        self.assertEqual(factorial(0), 1)
        self.assertEqual(factorial(1), 1)
        self.assertEqual(factorial(3), 6)

if __name__ == '__main__':
    unittest.main()
```

Automating API Endpoint Creation

Developers can use AI to generate API routes and handlers, accelerating backend development.

Example: AI-generated Flask API for a simple user database:

```python
from flask import Flask, jsonify

app = Flask(__name__)

@app.route('/users', methods=['GET'])
def get_users():
    users = [{"id": 1, "name": "Alice"}, {"id": 2,
"name": "Bob"}]
    return jsonify(users)

if __name__ == '__main__':
    app.run(debug=True)
```

Using AI to Debug and Optimize Code

Debugging is an essential part of software development, and AI can assist in identifying errors and optimizing performance.

AI Debugging Capabilities

- **Error Detection:** AI can analyze code and pinpoint syntax and logical errors.
- **Code Explanations:** AI tools provide detailed explanations of errors and suggest fixes.
- **Performance Optimization:** AI recommends ways to improve code efficiency and reduce execution time.

Example: AI-Assisted Debugging in Python

A developer encounters an issue where their function doesn't return the expected result:

```python
# Incorrect implementation

def sum_of_squares(n):
    total = 0
    for i in range(n):
        total += i ** 2
    return total
```

An AI debugger identifies that the function does not include n in the sum and suggests a fix:

```python
# Corrected function
def sum_of_squares(n):
    total = 0
    for i in range(n + 1):  # Fixed iteration range
```

```
    total += i ** 2
return total
```

Context-Aware Code Suggestions

AI code assistants provide **context-aware suggestions**, improving productivity by predicting what developers intend to write next. These tools analyze:

- **Programming patterns** from vast datasets.
- **Function and variable names** to generate relevant suggestions.
- **Project-specific code style** for consistency.

Example: Smart Code Completion

When writing a function to find the maximum value in a list, AI suggests the most common approach:

```
# AI-suggested function to find max value
def find_max(lst):
    return max(lst)
```

If additional constraints are required (e.g., ignoring negative numbers), AI can adjust suggestions based on context:

```
# AI-suggested function with filtering
def find_max(lst):
    return max([num for num in lst if num >= 0])
```

Conclusion

AI-powered code assistance is transforming software development by automating tasks, improving code quality, and accelerating debugging. By leveraging AI tools, developers can write cleaner, more efficient code while focusing on higher-level problem-solving. As AI continues to evolve, its role in software engineering will only become more integral, offering even more advanced capabilities in the future.

Chapter 4: Working with Different Programming Languages

Introduction

Cursor is designed to be a powerful AI-assisted coding tool that adapts to a wide range of programming languages. Whether you're working with Python, JavaScript, TypeScript, C++, or other languages, Cursor can help streamline development, improve code quality, and enhance productivity. This chapter explores best practices for using Cursor across different programming languages, how it adapts to various coding styles, and how to leverage AI-generated documentation and comments effectively.

Best Practices for Different Programming Languages

Python

Python is widely used for data science, web development, and automation. Cursor enhances Python development with:

- **Code suggestions**: Cursor provides intelligent autocompletions for functions, loops, and complex logic.

- **Style consistency**: Cursor ensures adherence to PEP 8 guidelines.
- **Refactoring assistance**: Suggestions for optimizing functions, reducing redundancy, and improving efficiency.
- **AI-generated documentation**: Automated docstrings and explanations for complex algorithms.

Example:

```
def fibonacci(n: int) -> int:
    """Returns the nth Fibonacci number."""
    if n <= 0:
        raise ValueError("n must be a positive
integer")
    elif n == 1:
        return 0
    elif n == 2:
        return 1
    return fibonacci(n - 1) + fibonacci(n - 2)
```

JavaScript

JavaScript is the backbone of web development. Cursor assists JavaScript developers by:

- **Autocomplete for ES6+ features**: Suggestions for modern syntax like arrow functions and async/await.
- **Linting and best practices**: Cursor integrates with ESLint to ensure cleaner, more maintainable code.
- **Debugging insights**: AI-generated explanations for common JavaScript errors.
- **Automated function descriptions**: Ensuring clear documentation and readability.

Example:

```
/**
 * Calculates the sum of two numbers.
 * @param {number} a - First number.
 * @param {number} b - Second number.
 * @returns {number} Sum of a and b.
 */
function add(a, b) {
    return a + b;
}
```

TypeScript

TypeScript extends JavaScript by adding static types. Cursor enhances TypeScript development through:

- **Type inference and suggestions**: Cursor ensures type safety by detecting potential issues early.
- **Conversion assistance**: AI helps convert JavaScript code to TypeScript.
- **Enhanced documentation**: Auto-generating JSDoc with type annotations.

Example:

```
/**
 * Fetches user data from an API.
 * @param {string} userId - The ID of the user.
 * @returns {Promise<User>} A promise that resolves to
user data.
 */
async function getUser(userId: string): Promise<User>
{
```

```
    const          response          =          await
fetch(`https://api.example.com/users/${userId}`);
    return response.json();
}
```

C++

C++ is widely used for system programming and high-performance applications. Cursor supports C++ with:

- **Memory management suggestions**: Helps avoid memory leaks and optimize performance.
- **Code refactoring**: Simplifies complex logic and improves readability.
- **Error explanations**: AI suggests fixes for common segmentation faults and memory issues.
- **Automated comments**: Generates explanations for complex algorithms and pointer usage.

Example:

```cpp
#include <iostream>

/**
 * Computes the factorial of a number.
 * @param n An integer number.
 * @return Factorial of n.
 */
int factorial(int n) {
    if (n == 0) return 1;
    return n * factorial(n - 1);
}

int main() {
```

```
    int num = 5;
    std::cout << "Factorial of " << num << " is " <<
factorial(num) << std::endl;
    return 0;
}
```

How Cursor Adapts to Different Coding Styles

Cursor is built to recognize and adapt to various coding styles based on:

- **Language-specific conventions**: Automatically applying best practices for different languages.
- **Custom user preferences**: Learning from user behavior to suggest personalized code improvements.
- **Project-specific guidelines**: Adapting to existing codebases and ensuring consistency.
- **Framework and library awareness**: Providing relevant suggestions for frameworks like React, Django, and more.

For example, Cursor might suggest `snake_case` for Python but `camelCase` for JavaScript, aligning with each language's best practices.

Using AI-Generated Documentation and Comments

AI-generated documentation ensures that code remains readable and maintainable. Cursor helps with:

- **Generating docstrings**: Automatically creating documentation for functions and classes.
- **Explaining complex logic**: Adding inline comments to clarify intricate algorithms.
- **Summarizing code sections**: Providing an overview of what each part of the code does.

Example:

```python
class BankAccount:
    """
    Represents a simple bank account with deposit and
withdrawal functions.
    """
    def __init__(self, balance: float = 0.0):
        """Initializes the account with an optional
balance."""
        self.balance = balance

    def deposit(self, amount: float):
        """Deposits a specified amount into the
account."""
        self.balance += amount

    def withdraw(self, amount: float):
        """Withdraws a specified amount from the
account if sufficient balance exists."""
        if amount > self.balance:
```

```
        raise ValueError("Insufficient funds")
    self.balance -= amount
```

Conclusion

Cursor is a versatile AI coding assistant that improves productivity across multiple programming languages. By understanding the unique best practices of each language, adapting to different coding styles, and generating AI-powered documentation and comments, Cursor helps developers write cleaner, more efficient, and well-documented code. Whether you're working with Python, JavaScript, TypeScript, C++, or another language, integrating Cursor into your workflow can significantly enhance your development experience.

Chapter 5: Enhancing Productivity with Cursor

Cursor is a powerful AI-powered coding assistant that can significantly enhance developer productivity by automating repetitive tasks, improving code quality, and streamlining workflows. In this chapter, we explore how Cursor can help developers optimize their work through AI-driven test case generation, automation of boilerplate code, efficient management of large codebases, and acceleration of software development workflows.

Using AI for Test Case Generation

Writing test cases is an essential yet time-consuming part of software development. AI-powered tools within Cursor can automatically generate test cases based on function definitions, reducing the effort required for manual testing. Here's how developers can leverage Cursor for test case generation:

1. **Automated Unit Test Creation:** Cursor analyzes function signatures and existing code to suggest appropriate unit tests, saving developers time and effort.
2. **Edge Case Handling:** AI can detect potential edge cases that might not be immediately obvious, ensuring robust testing coverage.
3. **Continuous Testing Integration:** Developers can integrate AI-generated test cases into continuous integration (CI)

pipelines, improving software reliability and reducing deployment risks.

By automating test case generation, developers can focus more on writing business logic rather than spending time creating exhaustive test scenarios.

Automating Boilerplate Code

Boilerplate code refers to repetitive, standardized code that is often required to set up projects, define classes, or interact with APIs. Cursor helps developers reduce redundancy by:

1. **Code Snippet Suggestions:** Cursor provides intelligent code suggestions based on project context, reducing the need for manual typing.
2. **Template-Based Code Generation:** AI-driven templates can quickly generate standard code structures for frameworks such as Django, Flask, or React.
3. **Autofilling Function Definitions:** Cursor predicts function implementations based on comments and naming conventions, accelerating development speed.

By automating boilerplate code, Cursor minimizes the need for redundant typing and enables developers to focus on implementing business logic.

Managing Large Codebases Efficiently

As projects grow in size, managing large codebases becomes increasingly complex. Cursor provides various features to help developers navigate and maintain large projects with ease:

1. **Smart Code Navigation:** Cursor offers intelligent search, allowing developers to quickly locate functions, classes, and variables across large repositories.
2. **Code Summarization:** AI-generated summaries help developers understand unfamiliar code sections without spending hours reading through documentation.
3. **Refactoring Assistance:** Cursor suggests improvements and best practices for restructuring code, enhancing maintainability and readability.
4. **Dependency Tracking:** AI analyzes dependencies and suggests optimizations to prevent unnecessary imports and reduce bloat.

With these capabilities, developers can manage large-scale software projects more efficiently, ensuring code remains clean and scalable.

Speeding Up Software Development Workflows

AI-driven tools like Cursor can significantly accelerate software development workflows by:

1. **Automating Code Reviews:** AI provides real-time feedback on potential issues, helping developers write cleaner, more efficient code.

2. **Enhancing Debugging Efficiency:** Cursor suggests possible fixes for errors and highlights problematic sections of code.
3. **Streamlining Documentation:** AI-generated comments and documentation ensure that code remains well-documented without additional effort.
4. **Seamless Collaboration:** Developers can integrate Cursor with version control systems like Git to improve code-sharing and team collaboration.

By leveraging these capabilities, teams can speed up their development cycles, reduce debugging time, and enhance overall productivity.

Conclusion

Cursor is a game-changing tool for developers looking to enhance productivity and streamline software development processes. From AI-driven test case generation to efficient code management and automation of repetitive tasks, Cursor empowers developers to work faster and more efficiently. By integrating these AI-powered features into their workflow, developers can optimize their coding experience and focus on innovation rather than routine tasks.

Chapter 6: Advanced Cursor Features

Real-Time Collaboration with AI-Powered Pair Programming

Cursor takes pair programming to the next level by integrating AI into the collaborative workflow. Developers can leverage AI-driven suggestions in real-time while working with teammates on the same project. Here are key aspects of AI-powered pair programming in Cursor:

- **Live Code Suggestions**: The AI offers context-aware code completions, bug fixes, and refactoring suggestions based on real-time changes.
- **Smart Merge Conflict Resolution**: When multiple developers work on the same file, Cursor assists in detecting and resolving merge conflicts efficiently.
- **Context-Aware Chat**: Users can ask the AI for explanations, code optimizations, and best practices while coding.
- **Seamless Cloud Sync**: Changes made by one developer are instantly available to others, reducing the need for manual code synchronization.

How to Enable AI-Powered Pair Programming in Cursor

1. Open Cursor and navigate to the settings panel.

2. Enable the **AI Pair Programming** feature under Collaboration.
3. Share the session link with your teammates.
4. Start coding together with AI-enhanced assistance.

Customizing AI Responses and Settings

Cursor allows users to tailor AI interactions to fit their development style and project requirements. Customization options include:

- **Adjusting AI Creativity**: Users can set the level of creativity for AI-generated suggestions. Higher creativity is useful for brainstorming solutions, while lower creativity ensures precise, predictable responses.
- **Prompt Engineering**: Developers can modify how the AI interprets their prompts to generate more relevant answers.
- **Code Style Preferences**: AI-generated code can be aligned with preferred formatting rules, ensuring consistency across the project.
- **Response Filtering**: Fine-tune AI outputs to focus on security, performance, or best practices based on project needs.

Steps to Customize AI in Cursor

1. Navigate to **Settings > AI Preferences**.
2. Adjust parameters such as creativity level, preferred languages, and response filtering.
3. Save your changes and test AI responses in a sample coding session.

Integrating Cursor with VS Code Extensions

One of Cursor's strengths is its compatibility with **VS Code extensions**, allowing developers to enhance functionality seamlessly. Some key integrations include:

- **Linting and Formatting**: Use extensions like ESLint and Prettier alongside Cursor's AI suggestions to maintain clean code.
- **Debugger Integration**: Connect Cursor with debugging tools such as the VS Code Debugger to analyze and resolve issues efficiently.
- **GitHub Copilot Coexistence**: Cursor can work alongside GitHub Copilot, allowing developers to compare AI-generated solutions and choose the best one.
- **Terminal and CLI Tools**: Enhance automation by integrating CLI tools within Cursor's AI environment.

How to Add VS Code Extensions in Cursor

1. Open Cursor and go to **Extensions Marketplace**.
2. Search for the desired VS Code extension.
3. Click **Install** and configure the settings as needed.
4. Restart Cursor to apply the changes.

Using Cursor for DevOps and Automation Scripts

Cursor is not just a development tool—it's a powerful asset for DevOps and automation scripting. With its AI capabilities, users can:

- **Automate CI/CD Pipelines**: Generate scripts for deployment automation, infrastructure as code (IaC), and monitoring tools.
- **Create and Optimize Bash Scripts**: AI can suggest, refactor, and debug shell scripts for system automation.
- **Enhance Cloud Deployment**: Integrate Cursor with cloud services like AWS, Azure, and Google Cloud to streamline infrastructure management.
- **Security Audits**: AI can analyze scripts for potential vulnerabilities and suggest improvements.

Example: Automating a Deployment Script with Cursor

1. Open Cursor and create a new shell script file (`deploy.sh`).
2. Type a comment explaining the script's purpose, such as:
3. `# AI-generated script for automated deployment`
4. Ask Cursor AI to generate a deployment script for a specific cloud provider.
5. Review and test the script in a staging environment before deployment.

Conclusion

Mastering these advanced features in Cursor enhances productivity and streamlines development workflows. By leveraging real-time AI collaboration, customizing AI responses, integrating VS Code extensions, and automating DevOps processes, developers can significantly boost efficiency and code quality.

Chapter 7: Debugging and Optimization with AI

Introduction

Debugging and optimizing code can be one of the most time-consuming aspects of software development. Traditional debugging methods often involve manually analyzing logs, tracing errors, and running tests, which can be slow and inefficient. However, AI-powered tools have transformed the debugging and optimization landscape, allowing developers to identify and fix issues more efficiently while improving overall code quality and performance.

In this chapter, we will explore how AI assists in detecting and fixing bugs faster, optimizing performance, and analyzing legacy code to improve maintainability and efficiency.

Detecting and Fixing Bugs Faster

AI-Powered Debugging Tools

AI-driven debugging tools have significantly enhanced the software development process by automatically identifying anomalies, predicting potential errors, and suggesting fixes. Some key AI-powered debugging tools include:

- **DeepCode**: Uses machine learning to analyze code and detect potential vulnerabilities and inefficiencies.
- **Codex (GitHub Copilot)**: Helps developers by suggesting corrections and improvements in real-time.
- **Microsoft IntelliCode**: Provides intelligent code completion and debugging assistance.
- **AI-based Log Analyzers**: Tools like Loggly and Splunk use AI to detect patterns and errors in log files automatically.

Automated Bug Detection

AI algorithms, particularly those using natural language processing (NLP) and machine learning, can analyze vast amounts of code to detect common bug patterns. AI-powered systems can:

- Identify **syntax errors**, **runtime errors**, and **logical inconsistencies**.
- Predict **potential security vulnerabilities** before they are exploited.
- Suggest **code refactoring** to prevent future errors.

AI-Assisted Debugging in Real-Time

Real-time AI-assisted debugging is becoming increasingly prevalent with IDEs integrating AI-driven debugging suggestions. These tools can:

- Highlight **suspicious code segments** before compilation.
- Automatically **generate test cases** based on previous error patterns.
- Offer **context-aware error explanations** and potential solutions.

Performance Tuning and Code Quality Improvement

AI for Performance Profiling

Performance bottlenecks in software can lead to inefficiencies and poor user experiences. AI-driven performance profilers analyze runtime behavior and provide actionable insights. Popular AI-powered profiling tools include:

- **Pyroscope**: Uses AI to analyze CPU and memory usage.
- **Google Cloud Profiler**: Detects performance issues in cloud-based applications.
- **Dynatrace**: An AI-driven APM tool that provides real-time performance monitoring and optimization.

AI-enhanced profiling tools:

- Monitor **CPU, memory, and network usage** to detect inefficiencies.
- Automatically suggest **code modifications** to improve speed.
- Identify **redundant or inefficient loops, queries, and algorithms**.

AI for Code Quality Enhancement

AI-powered tools not only optimize performance but also enhance code quality by enforcing best practices. Some AI-driven strategies include:

- **Static Code Analysis**: AI checks code for readability, maintainability, and adherence to coding standards.
- **Automated Code Reviews**: AI can review pull requests and suggest improvements before merging.
- **Self-Healing Code**: AI can refactor code automatically based on past patterns and best practices.

Popular tools for AI-driven code quality improvement:

- **SonarQube**: Detects code smells, vulnerabilities, and inefficiencies.
- **Codacy**: Provides automated code review and suggestions.
- **DeepCode**: Uses AI to identify and fix coding issues.

Using AI to Understand and Analyze Legacy Code

Challenges of Legacy Code

Legacy code is often difficult to maintain due to outdated programming paradigms, lack of documentation, and complex dependencies. AI has proven to be a valuable asset in analyzing and modernizing such systems by:

- **Reverse Engineering**: AI tools can interpret undocumented code and generate explanations.
- **Automated Documentation Generation**: AI-powered systems can extract logic from legacy code and create structured documentation.

- **Code Translation**: AI can help migrate legacy code to modern programming languages with minimal manual intervention.

AI-Powered Legacy Code Analysis Tools

Several AI-powered tools are designed to help developers understand and modernize legacy systems:

- **IBM Watson AI for Code Modernization**: Assists in translating and optimizing legacy codebases.
- **TransCoder (by Facebook AI)**: An AI-based model that converts code between different programming languages.
- **OpenRefactory**: Uses AI to refactor and improve legacy code quality.

Steps for AI-Assisted Legacy Code Optimization

1. **Code Scanning**: AI scans the entire legacy codebase to identify inefficiencies, unused code, and potential security vulnerabilities.
2. **Pattern Recognition**: AI detects recurring patterns and logic structures to improve readability and maintainability.
3. **Documentation Generation**: AI tools generate structured documentation to help developers understand complex codebases.
4. **Automated Refactoring**: AI suggests and applies modifications to modernize the code while preserving its original functionality.

Conclusion

AI-driven debugging, optimization, and legacy code analysis are revolutionizing software development by increasing efficiency, improving code quality, and simplifying maintenance. By leveraging AI-powered tools, developers can:

- Detect and fix bugs faster.
- Optimize code performance and ensure high-quality standards.
- Analyze and modernize legacy systems efficiently.

The integration of AI into debugging and optimization workflows not only enhances developer productivity but also ensures more reliable and efficient software solutions. As AI continues to evolve, it will play an even greater role in shaping the future of software development.

Chapter 8: Cursor for Web and Cloud Development

Introduction

In modern web and cloud development, AI-assisted tools have revolutionized the way developers build, test, and deploy applications. Cursor, an AI-powered code editor, enhances productivity by providing intelligent suggestions, real-time debugging, and automated deployment guidance. This chapter explores how to leverage Cursor for AI-assisted front-end development, full-stack application building, and AI-powered DevOps solutions.

AI-Assisted Front-End Development

Enhancing Development with AI

Front-end development involves creating user interfaces with frameworks like React, Vue, and Svelte. Cursor streamlines this process by:

- **Auto-generating UI components**: Cursor suggests complete UI elements based on context, reducing boilerplate code.

- **Predictive coding assistance**: Cursor predicts and autocompletes HTML, CSS, and JavaScript snippets, improving efficiency.
- **Debugging support**: The AI identifies and fixes common front-end issues in real time.

React with AI Assistance

React is a popular library for building dynamic UIs. Cursor enhances React development by:

- Suggesting component structures based on existing patterns.
- Generating reusable hooks and state management logic.
- Offering AI-driven accessibility improvements and responsive design suggestions.

Vue and Svelte Development

For Vue and Svelte developers, Cursor provides:

- **Vue.js Assistance**: AI-powered template suggestions, computed property optimizations, and Vuex store management.
- **Svelte Support**: Automated state handling, scoped styles generation, and compiler error fixes.

By leveraging Cursor's AI-powered insights, front-end developers can accelerate their workflow and maintain high code quality.

Building Full-Stack Applications with AI Guidance

Automating Back-End Logic

Full-stack development involves handling both client-side and server-side logic. Cursor aids in back-end development by:

- **Generating API endpoints**: Cursor can suggest RESTful API structures and GraphQL queries.
- **Database integration**: AI recommends optimized queries for databases like PostgreSQL, MongoDB, and MySQL.
- **Security enhancements**: Cursor flags security vulnerabilities and proposes best practices.

AI-Powered Framework Support

Cursor integrates seamlessly with popular full-stack frameworks like:

- **Next.js**: Automatic route generation, server-side rendering optimizations, and API handlers.
- **Node.js & Express**: AI-driven middleware recommendations, authentication setups, and request handling.
- **Django & Flask**: Suggested model relationships, ORM queries, and API responses.

Deployment Automation

Cursor simplifies deployment tasks with:

- **Containerization support**: AI helps create Dockerfiles and Kubernetes configurations.
- **CI/CD pipeline suggestions**: Cursor generates GitHub Actions, GitLab CI/CD scripts, and Azure DevOps configurations.
- **Serverless deployment**: AI provides AWS Lambda, Google Cloud Functions, and Vercel deployment guidance.

Deploying Projects with AI-Powered DevOps Suggestions

AI-Optimized Infrastructure Setup

AI-driven DevOps with Cursor automates cloud deployments by:

- Recommending best cloud providers (AWS, Azure, Google Cloud) based on project needs.
- Suggesting infrastructure as code (IaC) configurations with Terraform or AWS CloudFormation.
- Automating scaling strategies for high availability and cost optimization.

AI-Assisted Monitoring and Performance Optimization

Once deployed, applications require monitoring and performance tuning. Cursor assists by:

- **Analyzing logs**: AI detects anomalies in logs from platforms like ELK Stack or AWS CloudWatch.

- **Performance profiling**: Cursor suggests optimizations for database queries, API response times, and frontend load times.
- **Security audits**: AI scans for vulnerabilities, outdated dependencies, and compliance risks.

Continuous Deployment with AI-Powered Pipelines

AI simplifies the continuous integration and deployment (CI/CD) process by:

- Automating testing suites and performance benchmarks.
- Generating deployment scripts for Docker, Kubernetes, and cloud functions.
- Monitoring deployments in real time and recommending rollback strategies in case of failures.

Conclusion

Cursor revolutionizes web and cloud development by integrating AI into the entire development lifecycle. From front-end frameworks like React, Vue, and Svelte to full-stack applications and AI-powered DevOps, Cursor enhances productivity, reduces errors, and accelerates deployment. By leveraging Cursor's AI-driven suggestions, developers can create robust, scalable, and efficient applications faster than ever before.

Chapter 9: Real-World Projects with Cursor

Building a REST API with AI Assistance

Introduction

REST Apis serve as the backbone of modern web applications, enabling seamless communication between different services. With Cursor, you can leverage AI assistance to accelerate development, reduce errors, and ensure best practices. In this project, we will build a simple REST API using **Node.js and Express.js**, with AI guiding the coding process.

Step 1: Setting Up the Project

1. Open Cursor and create a new project directory.
2. Initialize a Node.js project:
3. `mkdir rest-api-project && cd rest-api-project`
4. `npm init -y`
5. Install dependencies:
6. `npm install express cors dotenv`

Step 2: Creating the API

1. Create an `index.js` file and import necessary modules:
2. `const express = require('express');`
3. `const cors = require('cors');`
4. `require('dotenv').config();`
5.
6. `const app = express();`

```
7. app.use(cors());
8. app.use(express.json());
9.
10. const PORT = process.env.PORT || 3000;
```
11. Define routes:
```
12. app.get('/api/message', (req, res) => {
13.     res.json({ message: 'Hello from AI-powered
    API!' });
14. });
```
15. Start the server:
```
16. app.listen(PORT, () => {
17.     console.log(`Server    running    on    port
    ${PORT}`);
18. });
```
19. Run the API:
```
20. node index.js
```
21. Test   with   Postman   or   a   browser   at
    `http://localhost:3000/api/message`.

AI-Powered Enhancements

- **Code Suggestions:** Cursor helps refine API structure and suggest improvements.
- **Error Debugging:** AI identifies potential runtime issues and proposes fixes.
- **Documentation:** AI can generate OpenAPI specifications automatically.

Automating Unit Testing and CI/CD Pipelines

Introduction

Automated testing and CI/CD pipelines ensure code quality and faster deployment. With Cursor's AI, you can streamline these processes efficiently.

Step 1: Writing Unit Tests

1. Install Jest for testing:
2. ```
   npm install --save-dev jest supertest
   ```
3. Create a `tests` directory and an `api.test.js` file.
4. Write test cases:
5. ```
   const request = require('supertest');
   ```
6. ```
   const app = require('../index');
   ```
7.
8. ```
   describe('API Tests', () => {
   ```
9. ```
       it('should return a message', async () => {
   ```
10. ```
        const         res         =         await
    request(app).get('/api/message');
    ```
11. ```
        expect(res.statusCode).toEqual(200);
    ```
12. ```
        expect(res.body.message).toBe('Hello
    from AI-powered API!');
    ```
13. ```
       });
    ```
14. ```
    });
    ```
15. Run the tests:
16. ```
    npm test
    ```

Step 2: Setting Up CI/CD with GitHub Actions

1. Create `.github/workflows/test.yml` and add:
    ```

```
2. name: Node.js CI
3. on: [push, pull_request]
4.
5. jobs:
6.   build:
7.     runs-on: ubuntu-latest
8.     steps:
9.       - uses: actions/checkout@v3
10.       - name: Setup Node.js
11.         uses: actions/setup-node@v3
12.         with:
13.           node-version: 16
14.       - run: npm install
15.       - run: npm test
```

16. Push changes to GitHub and check **Actions** for automated test results.

AI-Powered Enhancements

- **Test Case Suggestions:** AI generates test cases based on code structure.
- **Bug Fixing:** AI identifies errors in CI/CD and proposes solutions.
- **Workflow Optimization:** AI suggests best CI/CD practices for better performance.

AI-Powered Security Analysis for Code Vulnerabilities

Introduction

Security vulnerabilities can lead to data breaches and system compromise. Using Cursor's AI, you can analyze and secure your code effectively.

Step 1: Running AI-Based Code Analysis

1. Install a security scanning tool:
2. ```
   npm install --save-dev eslint eslint-plugin-security
   ```
3. Configure ESLint in `.eslintrc.json`:
4. ```
   {
   ```
5. ```
       "extends": "plugin:security/recommended",
   ```
6. ```
       "plugins": ["security"]
   ```
7. ```
   }
   ```
8. Run security analysis:
9. ```
   npx eslint .
   ```

Step 2: AI-Based Fixing

- **AI Suggestions:** Cursor flags potential vulnerabilities like SQL injection risks, improper authentication, and insecure dependencies.
- **Code Refactoring:** AI proposes better security practices automatically.

Step 3: Automating Security Checks in CI/CD

1. Update `test.yml` workflow to include security analysis:
2. `- run: npx eslint .`
3. Push to GitHub and ensure security tests run automatically.

AI-Powered Enhancements

- **Vulnerability Detection:** AI highlights security flaws in real time.
- **Automated Fixes:** AI generates secure code suggestions.
- **Continuous Monitoring:** AI integrates with security tools for proactive threat detection.

In this chapter, we explored how to build a **REST API**, automate **unit testing and CI/CD**, and leverage **AI for security analysis** using Cursor. AI-driven development significantly improves efficiency, security, and reliability in software projects. By incorporating these techniques, you can optimize your workflow and ensure high-quality code deployments.

Conclusion and the Future of AI-Assisted Coding

How AI Coding Tools Are Evolving

AI-assisted coding has already transformed software development, making it more efficient, accurate, and accessible. The evolution of AI in coding tools is driven by advancements in machine learning, natural language processing (NLP), and reinforcement learning. Modern AI tools like GitHub Copilot, DeepCode, and OpenAI Codex have demonstrated their potential by reducing boilerplate coding, suggesting efficient algorithms, and even debugging complex software.

Moving forward, AI coding tools will continue to improve in several key areas:

- **Enhanced Understanding of Context**: Future AI coding assistants will have deeper comprehension of project context, user preferences, and domain-specific requirements, leading to more precise suggestions.
- **Better Debugging and Optimization**: AI will not only detect bugs but also suggest fixes and optimize code for performance, security, and maintainability.
- **Seamless Integration with Development Environments**: AI will become more embedded in Integrated Development Environments (IDEs), cloud platforms, and DevOps pipelines, streamlining the entire software development lifecycle.

- **Adaptive Learning and Personalization**: AI-driven tools will learn from individual developers' coding styles, enabling more personalized recommendations and adaptive assistance.
- **Automated Documentation and Testing**: AI will play a bigger role in automatically generating meaningful documentation and robust test cases, improving software quality and maintainability.
- **Collaboration and Code Review**: AI will facilitate team collaboration by providing intelligent code review suggestions, detecting inconsistencies, and enhancing version control strategies.

Best Practices for Using AI Responsibly in Development

As AI coding tools become more powerful, developers must use them responsibly to ensure ethical, secure, and high-quality software. Here are some best practices:

1. **Verify AI-Generated Code**: AI-generated suggestions should be reviewed and tested thoroughly. Trust but verify to prevent potential security vulnerabilities and inefficiencies.
2. **Maintain Human Oversight**: While AI can automate many tasks, human judgment remains crucial. Developers should stay in control of architectural decisions and final implementations.
3. **Consider Ethical Implications**: AI-generated code should align with ethical principles, avoiding bias, unintended consequences, and security loopholes.

4. **Understand Licensing and Attribution**: AI-generated code may be derived from various sources. Developers should be aware of licensing constraints and intellectual property concerns.

5. **Keep Learning and Improving**: AI-assisted coding is a tool, not a replacement for programming skills. Developers should continue learning and refining their expertise to leverage AI effectively.

6. **Ensure Data Privacy and Security**: Avoid sharing sensitive or proprietary code with cloud-based AI tools unless necessary precautions are taken.

Next Steps: Exploring AI-Driven Software Engineering Trends

The future of AI-assisted coding is full of exciting possibilities. Developers should stay ahead by exploring emerging trends in AI-driven software engineering:

- **AI-Powered Code Synthesis**: Future AI systems may autonomously generate entire software applications based on high-level descriptions or requirements.
- **Self-Healing Code**: AI will enable software to detect and fix errors automatically without human intervention, reducing downtime and maintenance costs.
- **AI-Augmented DevOps**: AI will play a greater role in automating DevOps processes, from continuous integration (CI) to continuous deployment (CD), optimizing workflows and reducing manual effort.

- **Quantum Computing and AI**: As quantum computing advances, AI-assisted coding will help developers create quantum algorithms more efficiently.
- **AI-Driven Software Architecture**: AI will assist in designing scalable and resilient software architectures, recommending optimal frameworks and best practices.
- **Collaborative AI Coding Agents**: AI systems will become more interactive and collaborative, assisting multiple developers simultaneously in real-time pair programming environments.

Final Thoughts

AI-assisted coding is not just a trend; it represents the next evolutionary step in software development. While AI will enhance productivity and creativity, it is up to developers to guide its use responsibly. By staying informed, maintaining ethical standards, and continuously improving their skills, software engineers can leverage AI to create better, safer, and more efficient software for the future.

The journey of AI in coding is just beginning, and those who embrace it will be at the forefront of the next technological revolution.

Table of Contents :

Chapter 1: Introduction to Cursor 3

What is Cursor? 3

    Key Features of Cursor: 3

How Cursor Enhances Coding with AI 4

Cursor vs. Traditional Code Editors (VS Code, JetBrains, etc.) 5

Installing Cursor on Windows, macOS, and Linux 5

    Installing Cursor on Windows 6

    Installing Cursor on macOS 6

    Installing Cursor on Linux 7

    Post-Installation Setup 7

Conclusion 8

Chapter 2: Getting Started with Cursor 9

Setting Up Your Development Environment 9

    Step 1: Download and Install Cursor 9

    Step 2: Configuring Cursor for Your Workflow 9

    Step 3: Installing Extensions 9

Integrating Cursor with GitHub and Repositories 10

    Step 1: Connect Cursor to GitHub 10

    Step 2: Cloning a Repository 10

    Step 3: Committing and Pushing Changes 11

Understanding Cursor's AI Features 11

    AI-Powered Code Suggestions 11

    AI Code Explanation 11

AI-Powered Debugging 11

Customizing Cursor for Efficiency 12

Personalizing the Interface...12

Setting Up Shortcuts 12

Configuring AI Behavior 12

Chapter 3: AI-Powered Code Assistance...13

Writing and Refactoring Code with AI...13

Benefits of AI-Assisted Code Writing:...13

Popular AI-Powered Code Assistants:..14

Example: Generating a Function with AI 14

Generating Functions and Automating Repetitive Tasks....................14

Automating Unit Tests...14

Automating API Endpoint Creation..15

Using AI to Debug and Optimize Code 16

AI Debugging Capabilities 16

Context-Aware Code Suggestions 17

Example: Smart Code Completion 17

Conclusion...18

Chapter 4: Working with Different Programming Languages.............19

Introduction 19

Best Practices for Different Programming Languages......................19

Python..19

JavaScript...20

TypeScript 21

C++...22

How Cursor Adapts to Different Coding Styles 23

Using AI-Generated Documentation and Comments...........................24

Conclusion 25

Chapter 5: Enhancing Productivity with Cursor 26

Using AI for Test Case Generation...26

Automating Boilerplate Code 27

Managing Large Codebases Efficiently...28

Speeding Up Software Development Workflows 28

Conclusion 29

Chapter 6: Advanced Cursor Features 30

Real-Time Collaboration with AI-Powered Pair Programming..........30

How to Enable AI-Powered Pair Programming in Cursor.............30

Customizing AI Responses and Settings 31

Steps to Customize AI in Cursor 31

Integrating Cursor with VS Code Extensions 32

How to Add VS Code Extensions in Cursor................................32

Using Cursor for DevOps and Automation Scripts..........................33

Example: Automating a Deployment Script with Cursor 33

Conclusion 34

Chapter 7: Debugging and Optimization with AI 35

Introduction 35

Detecting and Fixing Bugs Faster...35

AI-Powered Debugging Tools 35

Automated Bug Detection 36

AI-Assisted Debugging in Real-Time...36

Performance Tuning and Code Quality Improvement 37

AI for Performance Profiling...37

AI for Code Quality Enhancement...37

Using AI to Understand and Analyze Legacy Code 38

Challenges of Legacy Code 38

AI-Powered Legacy Code Analysis Tools....................................39

Steps for AI-Assisted Legacy Code Optimization 39

Conclusion 40

Chapter 8: Cursor for Web and Cloud Development............................41

Introduction 41

AI-Assisted Front-End Development...41

Enhancing Development with AI..41

React with AI Assistance 42

Vue and Svelte Development..42

Building Full-Stack Applications with AI Guidance 43

Automating Back-End Logic 43

AI-Powered Framework Support 43

Deployment Automation...43

Deploying Projects with AI-Powered DevOps Suggestions 44

AI-Optimized Infrastructure Setup 44

AI-Assisted Monitoring and Performance Optimization 44

Continuous Deployment with AI-Powered Pipelines 45

Conclusion 45

Chapter 9: Real-World Projects with Cursor 46

Building a REST API with AI Assistance 46

Introduction 46

Step 1: Setting Up the Project..46

Step 2: Creating the API 46

AI-Powered Enhancements 47

Automating Unit Testing and CI/CD Pipelines 48

    Introduction 48

    Step 1: Writing Unit Tests 48

    Step 2: Setting Up CI/CD with GitHub Actions 48

    AI-Powered Enhancements 49

AI-Powered Security Analysis for Code Vulnerabilities 50

    Introduction 50

    Step 1: Running AI-Based Code Analysis 50

    Step 2: AI-Based Fixing 50

    Step 3: Automating Security Checks in CI/CD 51

    AI-Powered Enhancements 51

Conclusion and the Future of AI-Assisted Coding 52

How AI Coding Tools Are Evolving 52

Best Practices for Using AI Responsibly in Development 53

Next Steps: Exploring AI-Driven Software Engineering Trends 54

    Final Thoughts 55